CAN YOU
ESCAPE
THE MUMMY'S TOMB?

EARTHAWARE
KIDS

Written by Philip Steele
Designed by Tory Gordon-Harris
Edited by Kieron Connolly

EARTHAWARE
KIDS

Published by EarthAware Kids
Created by Weldon Owen Children's Books
A subsidiary of Insight International, L.P.
PO Box 3088
San Rafael, CA 94912
www.insighteditions.com

Weldon Owen Children's Books:

Publisher: Sue Grabham
Art Director: Stuart Smith
Assistant Editor: Pandita Geary

Insight Editions:

Publisher: Raoul Goff
Executive Director, Kids: Kate Jerome

ISBN: 978-1-68188-549-0

Manufactured in China

First printing, December 2020.

23 22 21 20 19 1 2 3 4 5

Picture Credits

Cover
Front: Sarcophagus (Paola Gallo/Shutterstock)
Back: Egyptian cobra (Eric Isselee/Shutterstock); statue of Anubis
(Metropolitan Museum of Art, New York); sand dunes (Nadia
Leskovskaya/Shutterstock)
Front and back: Hieroglyphs (artform/Shutterstock)

Inside Pages
Shutterstock
All pages: Hieroglyphs (artform); sacred dog (GoodStudio);
Multiple entries: 11, 13, 32, 68, 69 knife (Richard Peterson);
13, 46–47, 49, 51, 54, 56, 60, 66 oil lamp (J. Lekavicius); 16–17, 71
tomb interior (Cortyn)

Single entries: Title page coffin case (andersphoto); 4 mummy (Andrea
Izzotti); 5 pharaoh sarcophagus (Mikhail Zahranichny); 7 coffin case
(Jose Ignacio Soto); 8 cobra statue (Jaroslav Moravcik); 8–9, 71 harvest
mural (jsp); 10 Sah constellation (Ad_hominem); 10 Foreleg of Ox
constellation (angelinast); 10, 68 Sopdet constellation (angelinast);
17 grain harvest mural (jsp); 22-23 falcon figurines (Sergey-73);
22–23 small pyramid (Vladimir Zhoga); 22–23 sarcophagus (Mirko
Kuzmanovic); 24–25 sarcophagus face (N. Rotteveel); 26 Egyptian
cobra (Alberto Loyo); 30 cat statue (Tatiana.Do); 30 wardrobe (Orhan
Cam); 30 artifacts (Andrej Privizer); 30 jewelry (N. Rotteveel); 30–31
chariot (Jose Ignacio Soto); 30–31 statuette of Amun (Love Lego); 33
copy of Tutankhamun's throne (Jose Ignacio Soto); 36 Shu (Cholpan);
38 Valley of the Kings (Jeanette Teare); 41 mummy (CRM); 44–45 maze
(nissia); 52–53, 68 mummies (Jaroslav Moravcik, andersphoto Anton
Watman, Andrea Izzotti, PixHound); 55 tomb (Rafal Cichawa); 57 spear
(Bborriss.67); 62–63 room inside temple (Quintanilla); 66, 71 vulture
goddess and snake goddess relief (Thomas Wyness); 67 Deir el-Medina
(Rafal Cichawa)

Metropolitan Museum of Art, New York
12–13, 68 statue of Anubis; 16–17 Nakht's Offering Chapel; 20 false
door, Tomb of Metjetji; 23 vase, *shabti* box; 28, 69 scarab beetle amulet;
28, 69 ankh amulet; 29, 69 vases; 30-31 jars and amulets; 32 mirror;
42–43, 68 sarcophagus; 55 vases; 56 chisel; 58–59 Apep (Andrey0);
58–59, 71 Ra (airphoto.gr)

Alamy
10-11 Egyptian cosmos (The Print Collector); 19 bed from Tomb of Ka
(Realy Easy Star/Toni Spagone); 25, 34–35, 69 canopic jars (Prisma
Archivo Fotográfico); 31 board game (Cultural Archive); 48–49, 69 coffin
(Nerthuz); 51, 71 ostracon (Ahmed Gomaa/Xinhua/Alamy Live News);
60–61 Anubis weighing the heart (Lanmas)

Wellcome Collection
61 statue of Osiris (Science Museum, London. Attribution 4.0
International (CC BY 4.0)) 56–57, 68 fire drill (PSKOOK)

ESCAPE
THE MUMMY'S TOMB

Written by Philip Steele

STEP BACK IN TIME TO
ANCIENT EGYPT

ARE YOU READY TO TRAVEL MORE THAN 3,000 YEARS BACK IN TIME TO AN ANCIENT LAND OF PHARAOHS AND MUMMIES?

It is 1300 BCE, the time of Egypt's New Kingdom. Most of the land is a desert of sand and rock, shimmering in the heat. That is, apart from the river Nile. Without this precious lifeline, Egyptian civilization could not exist. All sorts of boats sail up and down the river, which provides water for people to drink and allows farmers to grow crops. On the green banks of the Nile, there are towns and cities with fabulous palaces and splendid stone temples. Inside the temples, priests make offerings to gods and goddesses.

Egypt is ruled by great kings and queens called pharaohs. People believe that the pharaohs have a direct link with their most important gods, such as Horus–the falcon-god, Ra–the Sun god, and Osiris–the lord of life and death.

When a pharaoh dies, his or her body is placed in a tomb on the edge of the desert. Pharaohs were once buried in huge pyramids, but in the New Kingdom they are buried in secret underground tombs in the valleys and the cliffs to the west of the city of Waset (Thebes).

MEDITERRANEAN SEA

LOWER EGYPT

RED SEA

Valley of the Kings

• Waset (Thebes)

UPPER EGYPT

River Nile

NUBIA

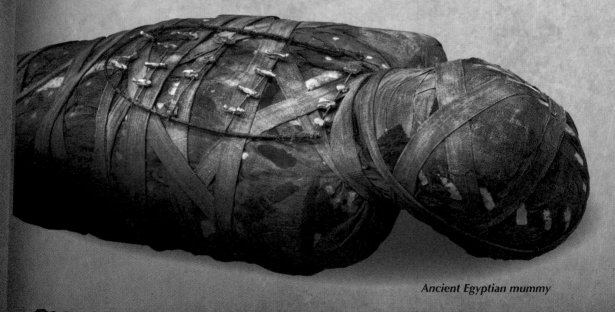

Ancient Egyptian mummy

The Egyptians believe that death is not the end, but a step on the way to the next world – the Kingdom of Osiris. Priests carry out religious rituals to make sure that the spirits of the dead pharaohs reach the next world safely. It is believed that if the priests make a single mistake, the world will end in darkness and chaos.

Egyptians believe that once a person has died, their spirit will need to return to their body, so it is preserved to look like it was when living. It is made into a mummy. The organs are removed and the body is dried in salts, stuffed, and wrapped in bandages. Pharaohs are buried with everything that they need for a safe journey into the next world. Food, drink, weapons, thrones, jewelry, chariots, and even favorite board games are left in the tombs.

A pharaoh's tomb is a fantastic treasure trove to behold. But it is also a place of magic and mystery, curses and danger. It is guarded by powerful gods and built to trap anyone who dares enter.

IN A FEW PAGES, YOU WILL FIND YOURSELF TRAPPED INSIDE A LONG-FORGOTTEN PHARAOH'S TOMB. DO YOU DARE TURN THIS PAGE?

Horus, the falcon god

WILL YOU TAKE THE
ESCAPE CHALLENGE?

WELL DONE, YOU ARE DARING AND BRAVE! GET READY TO ZOOM BACK IN TIME MORE THAN 3,000 YEARS TO THE LAND OF ANCIENT EGYPT.

Your character

You are 13 years old, and you live in the village of Set Maat near the great city of Waset (Thebes). Your father, Senbu, is a stonemason, who works every day building secret underground tombs in the royal burial ground that will become known as the Valley of the Kings. Senbu enjoys talking about his work, and you love to listen. You are fascinated by the mysterious tombs that protect the great mummified pharaohs. But you also know that the tombs are dangerous places – full of traps, curses, and magic and that they are protected by powerful gods.

How do you get trapped in a tomb?

It is another hot day, and your father has left for work. But he forgets to take his lunch! If you are quick, and take a shortcut through the Valley of the Kings, you might catch up with him. You are a fast runner, and you speed through the dust and the rocks. But as you turn a corner in the valley, you trip and fall. You try to regain your balance, but you find yourself falling down a shaft. If only you'd listened to your Mother's warnings to slow down!

HOW DO YOU ESCAPE?

1 Start at number 1. Read the story. Follow the arrow to the next number.

1
START
ROCKFALL!
Running too fast through the Valley of the Kings, you trip over a rock and hit the ground with a THUD . . .

▷ .... GO TO **93**

2 Read the next part of the story. Choose where to go next.

93
FROM 1.

WHERE ARE YOU?

You wake up and wonder where you are. Then you remember what happened. Above, you can barely see daylight – the top of the shaft is blocked with rocks and stones. Ahead of you is a wall made of mud brick, partly buried – but there's a large crack down the middle.

What do you do?

> Attempt to climb through the crack .... **GO TO** (109)

> Shout for help .... **GO TO** (130)

> Try to climb back up the shaft .... **GO TO** (98)

3 Read the clues carefully. They will help you to make your choices.

TOMB BUILDERS' TOOLS

To dig tombs out of the valley rockface, builders use many tools, including chisels and ropes. To light their way through the tunnels and caverns, they need a lamp, and to light a lamp, they need a fire drill.

Which things do you put in your bag?

> Rope, chisel, knife, lamp.............. **GO TO** (68)

> Rope, knife, fire drill, lamp .... **GO TO** (58)

> Rope, knife, comb, vase .... **GO TO** (13)

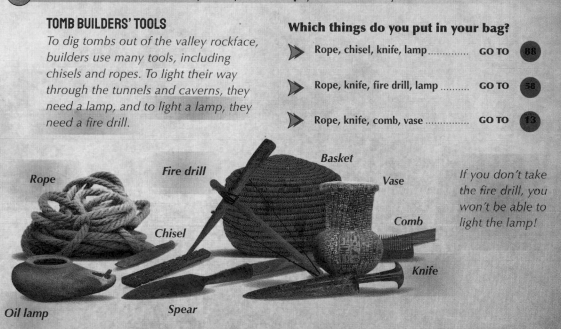

Rope
Fire drill
Basket
Vase
Chisel
Comb
Knife
Oil lamp
Spear

If you don't take the fire drill, you won't be able to light the lamp!

4 Ask the Eye of Horus.

When you see this symbol, use the wheel on the front cover to find out where to go next.

ASK THE EYE OF HORUS

Turn the wheel until you find the scarab beetle.

This reveals a number.

 **> 18**

Turn to step 18 to continue the adventure.

If you keep your wits about you, use all the clues, and make your choices wisely, you will escape the mummy's tomb. Turn the page if you dare.

ROCKFALL!

1

START

Running too fast through the Valley of the Kings, you trip over a rock and hit the ground with a THUD. Just as you begin to stand up again, the ground falls away beneath you and you seem to be falling down a shaft! You gasp and land with a bump.

Rocks are falling above you. You pass out.

▶ .... **GO TO** 93

WADJET'S WAY

2

FROM 127

You take the corridor marked with the cobra and soon reach a wall painting of a uraeus – a cobra with its head raised. This is a symbol of the goddess Wadjet that reminds you that Wadjet is the protector of Lower Egypt. That's a very long way away, and you feel as if you're getting farther from escaping the tomb. Perhaps you should have followed the corridor marked by Nekhbet, protector of Upper Egyptians like you. But ahead, something is glistening – could it be sunlight?

Do you?

▶ Continue along the corridor
towards the light .... **GO TO** 57

▶ Turn back to the corridor
marked by a vulture .... **GO TO** 100

PLOWING ON

3

FROM **18**

As you continue straight on, the corridor opens out to a room. Lifting your lamp, you see that it's decorated with beautiful paintings of farming scenes. The paintings remind you of home – how you'd love to be there now! It looks as if there are three corridors leading off from the other side of the room. You begin to approach them but STOP – there's a scorpion just inches away from your foot.

Do you?

➤ Step away from the scorpion, leave the room, and turn left into the annex .... GO TO 91

➤ Try to jump past the scorpion .... GO TO 21

FARMING

The Egyptians grow their crops along the banks of the river Nile. The yearly floods leave rich soil that is excellent for growing grain and vegetables.

DEATHSTALKER SCORPION

The deathstalker scorpion is one of the most dangerous scorpions. Its sting can cause severe pain and even death.

Father of the gods, Sah strides out across the sky.
His stars are the souls of dead pharaohs.

Sopdet is in this star pattern and the brightest star in the
night sky. She appears when the river Nile floods are due.

Tomb builders used Foreleg of Ox as a guide to build the
Great Pyramids along a north-south line.

GODDESS OF THE SKY

4

FROM **83**

You look for a way to climb up into the open night sky, but then realize that you're gazing at a ceiling. It is painted to look like the starry sky. You've been fooled by the goddess Nut! Her star-covered body arches over the ceiling. Nut must be a powerful goddess, because you can't take your eyes away from the stars. Perhaps if you count them, you can escape her hold over you.

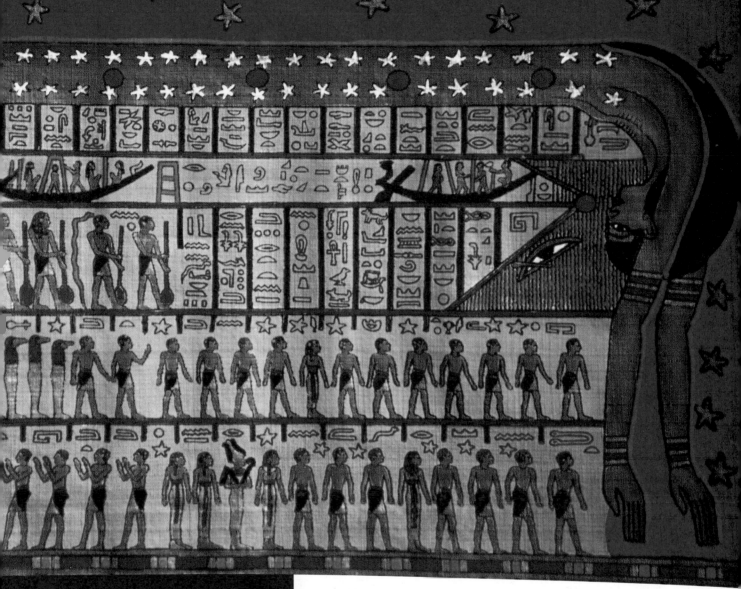

NUT

The power of the sky goddess Nut shields the pharaoh from harm and protects the mighty sun god, Ra.

Which constellation has an even number of stars?

▶ If you think it's Sah .... **GO TO** 34

▶ If you think it's Sopdet .... **GO TO** 80

▶ If you think it's Foreleg of Ox .... **GO TO** 99

A BRIGHT LIGHT

5

FROM **10**, **107**, **115**

Your knife cuts easily into the wall. You've soon made a hole and, holding up your lamp, you peer through. It's dazzlingly bright on the other side – is that sunlight? Is that the valley you can see? Can there really be just this one wall between you and escaping the mummy's tomb?

▶ .... **GO TO** 75

THE GUARD DOG

6

FROM 28, 89

Wriggling through the hole, you drop down onto the floor, landing badly and grazing your knee. But you dust yourself off and get back on your feet. Something moves in the shadows and makes you jump. Holding out your lamp, you come face to face with a huge dog's head. You leap back in shock. But wait – it's not really a dog's head. It's a statue of the god Anubis, the guardian of the burial chamber.

Do you dare to step past Anubis, the powerful god of the dead?

▶ No, Anubis is god of the dead, protector of graves and cemeteries. Anubis is dangerous. You turn back .... **GO TO** 113

▶ Yes, it's only a statue, and you've got to get out of here! .... **GO TO** 84

▶ Yes, but only after making an offering. You take out a honey cake from your father's lunchbox and leave it in front of Anubis .... **GO TO** 116

ANUBIS

Anubis is the god of mummies and tombs. Anubis helps decide whether people can enter the afterlife when they die. To please Anubis, people leave offerings of food and flowers at tombs.

BAD SEED

7

FROM 24

Are you sure the Eye of Horus said that it's the sowing season? Check again.

▶ .... **GO TO** 24

RAIDERS AGAIN

8

FROM 78

To avoid the tomb raiders, you slip back down to the bottom of the rope in the pit. You look up and see them leap across to the other side. They don't see you – or the rope.

▶ .... **GO TO** 108

FIRE! FIRE!

9

FROM **108**

You pull the plan out of your pocket
and look at it again in the lamplight.
But you're holding the lamp just a little
too close. Suddenly, the flame touches
the edge of the plan, setting it alight.
Flames races across the papyrus, and
you have to let go. Within seconds, all
that remains are some ashes falling
to the ground. Can you remember what
was on the plan?

 ASK THE EYE OF HORUS
Turn to the scarab beetle.

BREAKTHROUGH

10

FROM **23, 61**

You decide to put the amulets
back and immediately feel better.
Crossing to the other side of the room, you find
a clay wall. It doesn't look as if there's a way out.
But then you notice small holes in the wall.

What do you do?

▷ Use your knife to cut
a larger hole in the wall   **GO TO** 5

▷ Turn back the way you came –
you'll never get through there   **GO TO** 40

FLASH FLOOD

11

FROM **67**

The flash flood sweeps you along the winding corridor. Ahead, you can hear what sounds like a waterfall. It's too dark to see, but you guess that the water must be falling into a well. You desperately don't want to fall down any more pits, shafts, or wells. You reach your arm out above you, but you can hear that you're racing toward the well.

▶ ·················· **GO TO** 71

WHO IS THAT?

12

FROM **80**

The sarcophagus is creepy. You back away. But then you spot something even worse in the tomb – a human face! It isn't moving. You turn and run in the opposite direction.

▶ ·············· **GO TO** 68

FLASH FLOODS

Flash floods from heavy rains don't happen very often in the desert, but when they do, they race through the valleys and wash away buildings. Tombs are built with deep wells to catch floodwater so that it doesn't damage the burial chamber and the treasure room.

SCUTTLING SPIDERS

13

FROM **109**

With the rope, knife, comb, and vase in your bag, you begin to cross the storeroom. Your footsteps echo as camel spiders and scorpions scuttle across the floor. As you move forward, the way ahead gets darker and darker. Soon, it's too dim to see where you're going. You wish that you'd picked up the lamp and the fire drill!

Do you?

▶ Continue to feel your way along the walls .... **GO TO** 94

▶ Go back to get the lamp and fire drill .... **GO TO** 79

HERE THEY COME!

14

FROM **72**

You clamber back over the piles of treasure and up to the hole where you first entered the treasure room. You're just about to climb out when, from the other side of the wall, a man appears. He must be a tomb raider. Two other men join him and climb in. What should you do?

👁 **ASK THE EYE OF HORUS**
Turn to the Tyet symbol.

BUILDING UP

15

FROM **73**

You build a ramp out of the timbers in the pit and begin to climb up. But when you're only halfway your weight is too much. The ramp wobbles and slips away, and you fall back down to the bottom.

Do you?

▶ Try again to build a ramp .... **GO TO** 124

▶ Try to climb the walls .... **GO TO** 26

FIND A FLAME

16

FROM **88**

You try to light the lamp but realize you can't do that without the fire drill. You make your way back across the room in the darkness to collect the fire drill.

 ⟫ .... **GO TO** **126**

THE DOUBLE

17

FROM **59**

Wrong! It's the white crown.

⟫ .... **GO TO** **22**

A CHOICE OF DIRECTION

18

FROM **9**

Bad luck! Fortunately, you can remember a little bit of the plan from before it caught fire. There was a left turn into an annex in a cave or the chance to continue to another room.

Do you?

 ⟫ Continue straight on to a new room .... **GO TO** **3**

⟫ Turn left to the annex .... **GO TO** **91**

CARRY WHAT YOU CAN

19

FROM **52**

With your eyes feasting on the jewels and golden objects, you choose some treasures and open your bag. But to fit the treasures in, you'll have to take out the large fire drill. Will you need it again?

Do you?

⟫ Leave the treasures, because you might need the fire drill .... **GO TO** **59**

⟫ Take some treasures and leave the fire drill .... **GO TO** **65**

DARKNESS FALLS

20

FROM **119**

You open your bag and make an offering of the fire drill, leaving it on the altar. You really hope you're not going to need to light your lamp again. All seems good, but then there's a sudden breeze and your lamp goes out.

⟫ .... **GO TO** **33**

21 JUMP!
FROM 3

You jump past the scorpion, but its tail stings you. You hurry on but soon have to stop. Tired and dizzy, you sit down on the floor. Perhaps you shouldn't have tried to get past the scorpion. Perhaps you should have chosen a different path. Perhaps if – but you can't think clearly anymore…you pass out …

That's the end of your escape quest. You did well to make it this far through the tomb. Perhaps you'll make it out next time if you dare to start again.

▶ .... **GO TO** 1

22 THE ROYAL BED
FROM 17, 59, 96

Yes, the white crown is the crown of Upper Egypt. Let's hope that putting it on brings you luck in escaping the tomb. Next to the throne is a magnificent bed. You decide to rest for a moment, but you're so tired, you instantly fall asleep.

▶ .... **GO TO** 62

23 THE WARNING
FROM 61

Your head is still spinning, but you continue to move forward across the room. On the floor, you spot a fragment of pottery with some writing on it. You pick it up and read it. It's a warning from the tomb builders against taking anything, even a single pebble, from the tomb. Should you put the amulets back?

 ASK THE EYE OF HORUS
Turn to the symbol of Amenta.

BEDS
Beds are made of wood and sprung with strings of linen. Beds owned by the royal family can be gilded or carved.

THE SEASONS

In Egypt, there are three seasons — the flood season, the growing season, and the harvest season. During the flood season, no work is done in the fields. Instead, people are busy building palaces, temples, and tombs.

FLOOD SEASON

When the mighty river Nile floods, it spreads water and minerals onto the surrounding fields, leaving behind a rich layer of mud.

24

FROM **27**

THE CHAMBER OF HARVESTS

The ant bites are itchy, red, and angry, but you're sure that they'll clear up in a few days. You continue along the corridor and return to the room of the farming scenes. Each of the doorways leading off from the other side shows one of Egypt's three seasons. Which should you take? You think you should go through the door showing the season that you're in now, but you've been in the tomb so long, you can't think clearly. What were the farmers doing in the fields before you fell into the tomb? Were there even farmers in the fields?

ASK THE EYE OF HORUS

Turn to the shepherd's crook to find which doorway to take. If you see …

A sheaf for the
harvest season .... **GO TO** 56

A fish for the
flood season .... **GO TO** 127

A bowl of wheat for
the sowing season .... **GO TO** 7

GROWING SEASON

After the flooding of the river Nile comes the growing season, when crops are sown.

HARVEST SEASON

The Egyptians grow wheat to make bread and barley to make beer, as well as vegetables and fruit such as melons, pomegranates, and figs.

25

FROM 74

FINAL DASH

You start to run back into the tomb, but the tomb raiders grab you. They snatch the bag and lamp before dashing off. Now in complete darkness, you crawl in the opposite direction,

26

FROM 124

LAST CHANCE

You try to climb the walls of the pit, but neither your knife nor your fingers can get a good enough grip, and you soon slide back down to the bottom. You try again, but again you slide down. You keep trying until you're exhausted. You can't get out of the pit.

STOP THE PAIN!

27

FROM **46, 114**

As you climb up the rope, you feel another sting and then another before clambering over the edge of the pit. You relight the lamp and see that a whole army of fire ants has been attacking you.

Should you be worried and do something about the bites?

➤ Yes. Look for something
to soothe the pain .... **GO TO** 69

➤ No, continue .... **GO TO** 24

FIRE ANTS

Fire ant bites are painful and cause a red rash but for most people aren't serious. Their sting can be soothed with honey.

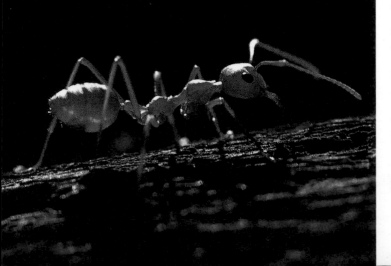

A FALSE DOOR

28

FROM **85**

You were brave to risk the rats, and it was worth it – they ran away! You climb over the rubble and find your way out of the maze. In front of you is a solid-looking stone door. You push against it, desperately thinking that it could be your way out. But the door won't shift. It is a false door, designed never to be opened. Holding up your lamp, you notice that part of the top of the door has cracked and broken away. It has left a hole, but the hole looks very difficult to reach.

What do you do?

➤ Use a rock to make a hole
in the bottom of the door .... **GO TO** 89

➤ Pull yourself up and crawl
through the hole in the door .... **GO TO** 6

SLIPPING FREE

29

FROM **39, 112**

The tomb raider finishes tying up you hands before joining the two others in gathering treasures. Once they have climbed back through the wall, you unclench your fists. That was a good trick your sister taught you! With your fists clenched, your hands are a little bigger, but when they're unclenched, there's a bit of slack in the rope. You pull your hands free. Then you untie yourself from the rest of the throne. You want to put as much distance as possible between yourself and the tomb raiders. You spot a small opening behind the bed. Should you crawl through?

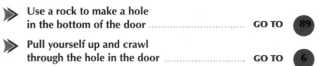

ASK THE EYE OF HORUS

Turn to the symbol of Ka.

FALSE DOORS

False doors are made of stone or wood. They look like real doors, but they can't be opened. The doors are a barrier between the living and the dead. It's believed that the dead person's spirit can pass through false doors.

RUBBLE AHEAD

30

FROM 91

You try to scramble across the rubble in the cave, but it's too difficult to balance yourself and hold up your lamp too. You'll never get across this way. You look back up to the ledge. Should you turn back or try to climb up onto the ledge?

ASK THE EYE OF HORUS

Turn to the symbol of Ba.

BACK TO THE PIT

31

FROM 44, 49, 101

Running your hands along the corridor wall in the darkness, you find your way back to the top of the pit. You loop your rope around the jutting rock and climb down. It's difficult, but at least you know now what to expect.

GO TO 81

32 FADING LIGHT

FROM 85

You continue on through the maze past the snakes, but one lunges and bites you. The bite hurts, but you keep walking. Soon you begin to feel dizzy and have to sit down. Your breathing becomes faint. You fall unconscious – and you don't wake up.

That's the end of your escape quest. You didn't get very far through the mummy's tomb!

▶ If you dare to start the adventure again .... **GO TO** ① 1

33 DANGER NEARS

FROM 20

Without the light from your lamp, you're in darkness. Then a glow appears in the distance. Your hopes rise – perhaps that's a way out – until you realize that it's the lamps of the tomb raiders approaching.

Do you?

▶ Call out for help – perhaps they'll help you this time .... **GO TO** 117

▶ Try to hide .... **GO TO** 50

34 ODDS OR EVENS

FROM 4

Are you sure there is an even number of stars in Foreleg of Ox? There are 7. Let's hope your other skills get you out of the mummy's tomb! Go back and count again.

▶ .... **GO TO** 4

35 A FACE IN THE DARK

FROM **110**

Peering inside the sarcophagus, you see that it's empty and sigh with relief. But you don't relax for long – you can sense that someone else is in the burial chamber. Lifting your lamp, you spot something across the room – a human face is looking at you. It isn't moving.

Do you?

➤ Run away .... GO TO 68

➤ Take a closer look .... GO TO 92

36 SLIPPING AND SLIDING

FROM **43, 90**

You try to climb the walls of the pit, but your fingers can't get a good enough grip, and soon you slide back down to the bottom. Do you think you can loop the rope around the jutting rock at the top of the pit?

ASK THE EYE OF HORUS
Turn to the Seshen flower.

37 DEADLY ERROR

FROM **125**

You jump past the cobra, but it lunges at you and bites. Hurrying on, you begin to feel sick and have to stop. You take out the piece of pottery again. You should have read the spell aloud *after* you were bitten. You want to read it aloud again now, but your vision is going blurry. You feel faint – and collapse.

That's the end of your escape quest. But you did well to make it this far through the tomb. Perhaps you'll make it out next time if you dare to start the adventure again.

➤ If you do .... GO TO 1

THE CASKET

38

FROM **47**

With the amulets placed in your bag, you step forward in the dim light. But the ground is uneven, and you trip and collide with a casket. Four jars fall out of it.

> .... GO TO **61**

TIED UP

39

FROM **82**

The tomb raider grabs you and drags you over to the throne. Pinning you down, he ties you to the throne and begins to tie your hands together.

Do you?

> Allow him to tie your hands, but clench your fists .... GO TO **29**

> Try to kick him out of the way .... GO TO **122**

ANOTHER WAY

40

FROM **10, 107**

Turning back from the wall, you swing your lamp around and notice a small, and very low, opening. You crouch down and crawl through.

> .... GO TO **115**

LETTING GO

41

FROM **86**

You let yourself drop down from the ledge, but you are surprised at how soft your landing is. What have you landed on?

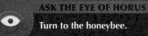

ASK THE EYE OF HORUS

Turn to the honeybee.

EXIT STRATEGY

43

FROM **106**

Before you can try to find the cave, you need to get out of the pit. You tuck the plan into your bag. At the top of the pit you can see a jutting rock – perhaps you could throw your rope up and loop it around the rock. Or the timbers on the ground around you could be used to build a ramp.

Do you?

> Try to climb the walls .... **GO TO** 36

> Build a ramp with the timbers .... **GO TO** 103

> Loop your rope around the rock .... **GO TO** 78

SNAKES

42

FROM **100**

The Eye of Horus instructed you to take the spell with you. Out of the corner of your eye, you now see a cobra slithering its way across the floor toward you.

Do you?

> Read out the prayer on the piece of pottery .... **GO TO** 125

> Carefully back away from the cobra .... **GO TO** 112

EGYPTIAN COBRA

The venom in a bite from an Egyptian cobra can stop you breathing and will kill you. There is no antidote.

GOING BACK

44

FROM **101**

Running your fingers along the walls in the darkness, you feel your way back up the steps. At last, you find the jars in the corridor. You hear the hiss of a snake. Perhaps it's in one of the jars. If you put your hand in to check for oil, the snake might bite you.

Do you?

➤ Dare to put your hand inside the jar .... **GO TO** 49

➤ Continue to the pit .... **GO TO** 31

➤ Go back to the jars in the treasure room .... **GO TO** 105

A SENSE OF TOUCH

45

FROM **88**

Feeling your way along the walls, you soon lose any sense of where you are. You want to light the lamp but realize that you can't do that without the fire drill. You make your way back across the room in the darkness to collect the fire drill.

➤ .... **GO TO** 126

INSECT BITES

46

FROM **114**

You slide back down the rope to the bottom of the pit. Getting out the fire drill, you light your lamp and see that you've been bitten by a fire ant. That's not too bad. You climb back up out of the pit.

➤ .... **GO TO** 27

47

FROM 92

LUCKY CHARMS

Across the burial chamber, something colorful catches your eye. You hold up your lamp and see two blue amulets. They are lucky charms, often wrapped up with mummies. You could certainly do with some good luck right now.

What do you do?

➤ Take the amulets with you – they might bring you luck. .... **GO TO** 38

➤ Leave them where they are .... **GO TO** 107

SCARAB BEETLE

The scarab beetle is a religious symbol of the rising sun and rebirth. Each day, as the sun rises, we start all over again as if we are reborn.

ANKH AMULET

The ankh is a popular lucky charm. It is a symbol of eternal life, which means living forever.

48

FROM 85

CLAMBERING ON

You clamber over the rubble and turn a corner in the maze. You can see dust falling in the light of your lamp. You look up just in time to see rocks crashing down on you. You've no chance of escaping and are buried under the rocks.

That's the end of your escape quest. You didn't get very far through the mummy's tomb!

➤ If you dare to start the adventure again .... **GO TO** 1

49

FROM 44

REACHING IN

You put your hands inside the jars. Nothing bites you; but the jars don't contain any oil, either. You're going to have to search elsewhere.

Do you go back ...?

➤ To the pit to check the jars there for oil .... **GO TO** 31

➤ To the jars in the treasure room .... **GO TO** 105

50 ALL ALONE

FROM 33

You try to hide behind the altar, but the tomb raiders barge into the hall and quickly find you. They haul you to your feet, grab your bag, and race off into the depths of the tomb. Now you're left in complete darkness with nothing.

GO TO 121

51 A GIFT FROM THE DEAD

FROM 97

The floor of the pit is sandy. Looking around, you see that it is littered with builders' rubble, timbers, and some pottery jars. And then you step back in shock – there's a skeleton. You shiver. Was this a tomb raider who fell into the pit long ago? Its hand is clutching a rolled-up piece of papyrus. Edging closer, you gingerly reach out your arm, making sure that you don't touch the skeleton. Then you slide the papyrus out of the skeleton's bony grasp and unroll it. Can this really be a plan of the tomb?

ASK THE EYE OF HORUS
Turn to the ladder.

JARS

In tombs, oil, wine, and food are often left for the pharaoh's journey to the next world. The contents of most jars soon dry up.

52

FROM **75**

FINDERS, KEEPERS

You cut a larger hole and crawl into the treasure room, clambering over baskets, boxes, jars, and chests. You're now surrounded by unimaginably beautiful items – golden cabinets, a chariot, ornaments, statuettes, musical instruments, and even board games.

Do you?

▷ Fill your bag with as many treasures as you can carry .... GO TO **19**

▷ Leave the treasures where they are .... GO TO **59**

TOMB TREASURE

People who are caught stealing tomb treasures can be put to death. They might be impaled on a stake or burned alive. Many tomb robbers get away with their crime but might still be cursed by a priest.

BARE HANDS

53

FROM **64**, **129**

With no tools but your bare hands, you pull away at the mud brick of the tomb wall. It's hard work, and your fingers are soon cut and bloody. But gradually, the hole gets larger. When it's big enough, you crawl through.

➤ ·············· **GO TO** 70

ALONG THE LEDGE

54

FROM **30**, **91**

You climb up onto the high ledge. It's so narrow that you have to shuffle your feet along sideways and cling to the rock with your hands to steady yourself. Thankfully, the ledge broadens out. But there's something blocking the path ahead. In the flickering flame of your lamp, you think you see a shriveled hand and a twisted foot. You shuffle forward and come face to face with . . .

➤ ·············· **GO TO** 102

YOU'RE ARMED

55

FROM 72

You shout out that you have a knife and hope that that will keep the tomb raiders away. Seconds later, three men climb through the hole that you made in the wall. The tomb raiders weren't frightened by your little threat at all. They are dazzled by the treasures, but what will they do to you?

➤ .... **GO TO** 82

BAD HARVEST

56

FROM 24

Are you sure that the Eye of Horus said it's the harvest season? Check again.

➤ .... **GO TO** 24

ON THE WALL

57

FROM 2

You continue along the corridor marked by Wadjet, getting nearer the distant light. Finally, you reach it, but it's not sunlight at all. It's a hand mirror reflecting your own lamp. The corridor is a dead end. You'll have to return and take Nekhbet's corridor.

➤ .... **GO TO** 100

HAND MIRROR
The Egyptians take great care of their appearance, and both men and women wear makeup.

INTO THE DARKNESS

58

FROM 109

With everything in your bag, you begin to cross the storeroom. Your footsteps echo as scorpions and camel spiders scuttle across the floor. As you move forward, the way ahead gets darker and darker. Soon, it's too dim to see where you're going. You rummage in your bag and pull out the lamp and fire drill. It's good that you remembered the fire drill, because you wouldn't be able to light the lamp without it!

➤ .... **GO TO** 126

59 PHARAOH FOR A DAY

FROM **19, 52**

Walking among the piles of treasure, you marvel at the precious stones and carved woods. You stop at a splendid golden throne and a pile of crowns. You can't resist sitting on the throne for a moment and wonder about trying on the crowns. There are crowns for different parts of Egypt. If you put on the crown for Upper Egypt, where you live, will it bless you in finding a way home?

ASK THE EYE OF HORUS

Turn to the vulture. If you see . . .

> The white
> crown .... GO TO 22

> The double
> crown .... GO TO 17

> The red
> crown .... GO TO 96

60 DIM LIGHT

FROM **77**

You scramble away from the mummies and begin to climb across the rubble to reach the edge of the cave, but it very quickly gets too dark without your lamp. You look up at your lamp on the ledge. You are going to have to climb back up there.

> .... **GO TO** 66

61

FROM **38**

FOUR SPOOKY JARS

Each of the four jars inside the casket is sealed tight – and it's just as well, because you know that these aren't just any kind of jar. They contain the sacred remains of the dead pharaoh's stomach, intestines, lungs, and liver! There is powerful magic surrounding these canopic figures. You're horrified that you bumped into the casket. Your head is now whirling, and you have a strange feeling in the pit of your own stomach. Have you been cursed because you took the amulets?

What do you do?

▶ You don't believe in curses,
so you keep the amulets .... **GO TO** 23

▶ You put the amulets back
where you found them .... **GO TO** 10

CANOPIC JARS

When mummies are made, some organs of the body are removed and placed inside special jars. The jars are designed to look like the four sons of the god Horus: Qebehsenuef, Duamutef, Imsety, and Hapy.

*Hapy
Protects
the lungs*

*Duamutef
Protects the
stomach*

WOKEN FROM A DREAM

62

FROM **22, 72**

Suddenly, voices in the tomb wake you up. Who are they? Are they a search party looking for you? Or perhaps they're dangerous tomb raiders?

Do you?

➤ Keep quiet and listen .... **GO TO** 72

➤ Call out for help .... **GO TO** 111

*Qebehsenuef
Protects the
intestines*

*Imsety
Protects
the liver*

A HANGING ROCK

63

FROM **29, 95**

The Eye of Horus has instructed you to crawl through the low opening. As you do, you keep your eye on a sharp rock jutting out just above your head. You don't want to cut yourself on that. But with all your attention focused on the danger above you, you fail to spot an open pit in the floor right in front of you – and fall right in.

➤ .... **GO TO** 97

SHOUTING OUT

64

FROM **128**

You cry for help, but no one answers and no one comes. Are you going to have to dig your way out?

ASK THE EYE OF HORUS
Turn to the Akhet symbol.

SHU'S REVENGE

65

FROM **19**

With your bag laden with treasures, you admire the beautiful objects in the treasure room. As you hold your lamp up to a wall painting of Shu, the god of the wind, a sudden current of air rushes through the room. Your lamp flickers and goes out. You're in complete darkness. Is this Shu's revenge because you took the pharaoh's treasure? Should you go back and find the fire drill?

ASK THE EYE OF HORUS
Turn to the Maat feather.

SHU
Shu, the god of the wind, is often shown with four ostrich feathers on his head.

END OF THE CAVE

66

FROM **86**

You use all your strength to pull yourself back onto the ledge. With a big sigh of relief, you pick up the lamp and push past the mummies. The ledge slopes down to the edge of the cave. You hope that this path will lead you out to the cliffs and the open air. At last, you reach the end of the cave, but there is no way out. With a sinking feeling, you realize that your only option is to climb back up the ledge and struggle back past the mummies to the main tomb itself.

▶ .... GO TO 101

APEP'S PATH

67

FROM **112**

The door marked by Apep leads you downward. You notice a distant rushing noise coming from above. Suddenly, a torrent of water surges toward you. It must be from a flash flood in the valley. The torrent knocks you off your feet, but you manage to hold your lamp up in the air.

▶ .... GO TO 11

THE GATEWAY GOD

68

FROM 12, 35

Turning from the human face, you run the other way and straight into a horrible wall carving of a person with a crocodile's head. It gives you the shivers. This is a gateway god, who guards the gates of the underworld. Which is worse – continuing beyond this strange beast or going toward the human face across the room?

ASK THE EYE OF HORUS

Turn to the crocodile. If you see . . .

> A human face   **GO TO** **92**

> A crocodile head .... **GO TO** **104**

GOD OF THE GATES

Priests believe that a dead person's spirit needs to pass through many sacred gateways to reach the underworld. The number of these invisible gates varies, but each is guarded by a god, a goddess, a spirit, or a monster.

SOME HONEY

69

FROM 27

To soothe the pain of the fire ant bites, you take another honeycake out of your father's lunch box and rub some of the honey on the bites. That feels a little better.

> .... **GO TO** **24**

70

FROM **53**

THE VALLEY OF THE KINGS

You're outside and back in the Valley of the Kings. In the distance, you can see your father and sisters looking for you. You shout out to them. They see you and wave back. You have escaped the mummy's tomb!

DRAGGED AWAY

71

FROM **11**

As the water carries you toward the well, you wave an arm around in the air, trying to find something to grab onto. Finally, you manage to grip the wall. With all your strength, you hang on while the waters tries to drag you away. When the water is just a trickle, you stand up, check your bag and lamp, and begin to stagger back up to the corridor. Where was the door marked by Ra?

ASK THE EYE OF HORUS
Turn to the turtle.

STRANGE VOICES

72

FROM **62**

The voices are coming from behind a wall. You creep closer to hear what they're saying. It's three people, at least. They're talking about how to share out the gold – they're definitely tomb raiders. Backing away, you trip over and make a thud as you hit the dusty floor. The voices suddenly stop. They've heard you.

What do you do?

➤ Shout out that they should stay away .... **GO TO** 55

➤ Hide behind the bed .... **GO TO** 95

➤ Leave quickly and climb back out of the treasure room .... **GO TO** 14

HELP AT LAST?

74

FROM **119**

You make an offering of your father's lunch, leaving it on the altar. Suddenly, you hear voices. It's the tomb raiders.

What do you do?

➤ Try to run back to the tomb .... **GO TO** 25

➤ Hide behind the altar .... **GO TO** 128

STUCK IN THE PIT

73

FROM **103, 118**

You're stuck at the bottom of the pit with no rope.

What do you do now?

➤ Build a ramp with the timbers around you .... **GO TO** 15

➤ Try to climb the walls .... **GO TO** 124

TREASURE ROOM

When Egyptians die, they are buried with possessions that they might use in the next world. The tombs of pharaohs are often packed with grave goods made of gold, silver, precious stones, and fine wood.

A GLINT OF GOLD

75

FROM **5**

No, that's not sunshine coming through the wall of the burial chamber. It's light being reflected from solid gold! You're looking into the treasure room, where the most precious grave goods are stored for use by the pharaoh on his or her way to the next world.

GO TO 52

STUMBLING

76

FROM **65**

Without your lamp, and stumbling in the darkness, you feel your way back to where you left the fire drill. At last, you find it. With all your concentration, you manage to work the fire drill in the dark. Then you relight the lamp. You take the treasures out of the bag and put the fire drill back in. From now on, you tell yourself, you'll leave the pharaoh's treasures in the treasure room, where they belong.

GO TO 59

TRAPPED

77

FROM **41**

With just a distant light from your lamp, you can't at first make out what you've landed on. But as you become more accustomed to the darkness, you see an eye. Then another. In fact, there are eyes and arms and legs all around you. You've landed in the middle of the mummies that fell off the ledge! You scream and try to jump up, but it feels as if the mummies' arms are holding you down.

.... **GO TO** 60

ROPE TRICKS

78

FROM **36, 43**

Throwing the rope up several times, you finally manage to loop it around the jutting rock. Then you snuff out the lamp and put it into your bag. You begin to climb the rope. When you're almost at the top, you hear the tomb raiders' voices again – and they seem to be getting closer.

Do you?

➤ Hang silently until they've gone .... **GO TO** 118

➤ Slip back down to the bottom of the rope .... **GO TO** 8

THE WAY BACK

79

FROM **13**

Turning around in the darkness, you cling to the wall as you make your way back. Gradually, it gets lighter and finally you can see the objects in the storeroom that you left. You leave the vase and chisel and pick up the lamp and fire drill.

➤ .... **GO TO** 126

A BROKEN SARCOPHAGUS

80

FROM **4**

You correctly chose the star pattern Sopdet and are free of Nut's hold over you. Relieved, you notice a huge stone sarcophagus in the center of the burial chamber. This is the resting place of a great pharaoh. The lid has been lifted, and the sarcophagus is open. You tiptoe closer . . .

Do you dare to look inside?

➤ Yes .... **GO TO** 110

➤ No .... **GO TO** 12

SARCOPHAGUS
A pharaoh's mummy is put inside a coffin, which is put inside a stone sarcophagus. The sides of the sarcophagus are inscribed with prayers for the dead. This is the most sacred place in the tomb.

SEARCHING FOR OIL

81

FROM **31**

At the bottom of the pit, you feel around you until you find the jars. Cautiously, you put your hand in each of them. They're all empty – apart from one. It's lamp oil! You refill your lamp and put it in your bag, ready to climb back up.

➤ .... **GO TO** 114

RAIDERS

82

FROM **14**, **55**, **111**

You move away from the jewels and ornaments. Two of the tomb raiders begin to stuff treasures into their bags. The third approaches you, unlooping a rope as he advances. Terrified, you back away toward the pharaoh's bed.

Do you?

➤ Freeze, hoping he'll leave you alone ..... **GO TO** 39

➤ Try to escape .... **GO TO** 87

LOOK UP!

83

FROM **116**

What a relief – you're in the burial chamber of a good pharaoh! Adjusting to the light, you look around. As you gaze up, you notice that there are stars twinkling above you. It's the night sky! The good pharaoh has blessed you with a way out. At last, will you be able to escape?

ASK THE EYE OF HORUS
Turn to the Seba star.

THE CRASH

84

FROM **6**

You pass Anubis without making an offering and begin exploring the burial chamber. But what's that rumbling sound above you? You look up just as a large section of the ceiling comes crashing down right on top of you.

That's the end of your escape quest. You didn't get very far through the mummy's tomb!

If you dare to start the adventure again . . .

➤ .... **GO TO** 1

THE MAZE

85

FROM **126**

The opening in the wall leads into a narrow corridor that branches left and then right, and then left again. Soon, you hardly know if you are coming or going! You remember your father telling you that tomb builders make the tombs difficult to navigate to try to fool any tomb raiders who hope to steal from them.

Finally, the corridor leads to three doorways, but which one should you take – A, B, or C? You can either take a guess or seek the help of the Eye of Horus.

ASK THE EYE OF HORUS
Turn to the symbol of the Shen to find out where to start.

RATS
Rats are more scared of you than you are of them. They will bite you only if they are cornered. The bite won't kill you, but you might develop a nasty infection.

Your way is blocked by a pile of rubble and there are rats climbing all over it.

If you want to dig your way through .... **GO TO** **28**

You reach a nest of snakes. They look like vipers.

If you are prepared to step over the snakes .... **GO TO** 32

Rocks block the corridor, and a skeleton is half buried in the rubble.

If you want to continue .... **GO TO** 48

EGYPTIAN HORNED VIPER
A bite from the venomous Egyptian horned viper will make you swell up, vomit, and bleed. Some bites will kill you.

86
FROM 102

HANGING ON

As you push past the mummies, part of the ledge crumbles. Some mummies drop to the rubble below, while others fall toward you. You leap back from the horrible faces, but the ledge is too narrow! You slip, dropping your lamp. The lamp lands safely on the ledge, but you fall – only just managing to hold on with your fingertips.

Do you?

➤ Try to pull yourself back up onto the ledge .... **GO TO** 66

➤ Let go and fall down to the rubble below .... **GO TO** 41

88
FROM 109

TOO DARK TO SEE

With the rope, knife, chisel, and lamp in your bag, you begin to cross the storeroom. Your footsteps echo as scorpions and camel spiders scuttle across the floor. The way ahead gets darker and darker as you move forward. Soon, it's too dim to see where you're going.

How do you find your way?

➤ Feel your way along the walls ...... **GO TO** 45

➤ Try to light the lamp .... **GO TO** 16

87
FROM 82

TAKING A DIVE

To escape, you run to the other side of the room. You're in luck! There's a low opening behind the bed. You seize the opportunity and dive through. But it's not a soft landing on the other side. In fact, it's not a landing at all – you're falling. Where are you going?

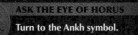

ASK THE EYE OF HORUS

Turn to the Ankh symbol.

89 BLOCKED

FROM 28

You try to use a rock to smash a hole in the bottom of the door but make no progress. You're going to have to pull yourself up and crawl through the hole in the top of the door.

> .... GO TO 6

90 CLIMBING HIGH

FROM 103

You begin to climb the ramp, but when you're only halfway up, your weight is too much. The ramp wobbles and slips away, and you fall right back down to the bottom of the pit.

Do you?

> Try to loop your rope around the rock at the top of the pit .... GO TO 78

> Try to climb up the walls .... GO TO 36

91 ENTER THE ANNEX

FROM 18

Turning left, the steps now go downhill into natural rock. The corridor opens out into a cave. It has been used as a dump and is piled high with rubble and coffin cases. It might be a shortcut to escape the tomb, but it looks difficult to cross. Then you notice a ledge running around the edge of the cave, but it's very narrow and a long way up.

Do you?

> Try to scramble across the rubble .... GO TO 30

> Climb up on to the ledge to cross the cave .... GO TO 54

MYSTERY OF THE COFFINS

FROM 68, 35

Taking a closer look at the face in the dark, you see that it's the pharaoh staring right up at you! Your whole body shakes in fear. Then you realize that it's the pharaoh's face painted on the top of his coffin. But the pharaoh's mummy will be inside! Tomb raiders looking for treasure must have lifted the coffin out of the sarcophagus.

 **GO TO** 47

WHERE ARE YOU?

FROM 1

You wake up and wonder where you are. Then you remember what happened. Above, you can barely see daylight – the top of the shaft is blocked with rocks and stones. Ahead of you is a wall made of mud brick, partly buried – but there's a large crack down the middle.

What do you do?

> Attempt to climb through the crack .... **GO TO** 109

> Shout for help .... **GO TO** 130

> Try to climb back up the shaft .... **GO TO** 98

COFFIN CASES
Coffin cases are shaped like the body of the person they're carrying, whose face is painted on the outside.

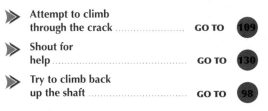

THINK AGAIN

94 FROM **13**

Feeling your way along the walls, you begin to lose any sense of where you are. You realize that you're going to have to go back and fetch the lamp and fire drill. You cling to the wall as you find your way back to the storeroom. As it gets lighter, you can finally see the objects that you left. You pick up the lamp and fire drill but now have no room in your bag for the vase and comb as well, so you leave those behind.

> .... **GO TO** 126

A HIDDEN OPENING

95 FROM **72**

Hiding behind the bed in the treasure room, you notice a low opening that you hadn't seen before. Should you crawl through?

ASK THE EYE OF HORUS
Turn to the papyrus stem.

THE RED

96 FROM **59**

Wrong! It's the white crown.

> .... **GO TO** 22

DOWN THE PIT

97

FROM **63, 87**

You land with a bump. Luckily, the floor is sandy. But where are you? In a pit? Another tomb? By some miracle, your lamp has stayed alight. Perhaps the gods blessed you for respecting the pharaoh's treasures. But how are you going to get out? It's ten feet or more up a sheer vertical wall back to the corridor.

▶ .... **GO TO** (51)

A WAY OUT?

98

FROM **93**

You try to climb up the shaft but soon see that it's blocked higher up with rocks from the rockfall.

Do you?

▶ Attempt to climb
through the crack .... **GO TO** (109)

▶ Shout for help .... **GO TO** (130)

EVENS OR ODDS

99

FROM **4**

Are you sure there is an even number of stars in Sah? There are 19. You're going to need to concentrate to get out of the mummy's tomb. Go back and count again.

▶ .... **GO TO** (4)

PITS

Deep pits are dug in many burial sites. Some are tombs. Some might be drains to stop damage from flooding, and some are there to stop tomb raiders reaching the treasure room and burial chamber.

THE SPELL

100

FROM 2, 127

You walk down Nekhbet's corridor and stub your toe on something. You crouch down to pick it up. It's a piece of pottery with a prayer written on it. The prayer is to be said aloud after you have been bitten by a snake. It might be useful later. Should you put the piece of pottery in your bag?

ASK THE EYE OF HORUS

Turn to the Menat symbol.

SPELLS

Like all Egyptians, tomb builders are superstitious and believe in magic spells. They write spells against bites and stings on old pieces of pottery.

OUT OF FUEL

101

FROM 66

You retrace your steps past the mummies, climb off the ledge, and leave the cave. You reach the corridor and turn off into a room with farming scenes painted on the walls. Three doorways lead out from the other side, but before you can approach them, your lamp flickers and goes out. It has run out of oil! With no oil, you can't relight the lamp. Where did you see jars that might have lamp oil in them? You remember seeing them in the corridor, the pit, and the treasure room.

Where do you go to look for oil?

⟩ The jars in the corridor .... **GO TO** 44

⟩ The pit .... **GO TO** 31

⟩ The treasure room .... **GO TO** 105

MUMMIES

A mummy is a dead body that has been preserved in chemicals and wrapped in cloth. To make a mummy, a hook is used to pull the brains out through the nose. The heart is left, but other organs are taken away and put inside canopic jars.

102

FROM **54**

MEET THE DEAD

… A pile of mummies! Some of them are still in closed coffin cases, but others have fallen out with their bandages trailing. You remember hearing that mummies are moved to different tombs to be stored if their own tomb is damaged. Their shrunken faces seem to be staring at you. You shiver in fear. Will this be the end for you?

Do you?

▶ Push past the mummies .... **GO TO** 86

▶ Jump off the ledge onto the rubble below .... **GO TO** 120

PILING UP PLANKS

103

FROM 43

You pick up the planks and wedge them against the wall of the pit. You're very pleased with your work!

GO TO 90

DOUBLE-CHECK

104

FROM 68

The Eye of Horus has instructed you to move closer to the gruesome god of the gates. Or has it?

GO BACK TO 68

105

FROM **44**, **49**, **101**

BLOCKED PATH

In the darkness, you retrace your steps to the top of the pit. You take out your rope, tie it around the jutting rock, and swing across. You reach the other side and feel around in the darkness for the low opening to the treasure room. But all you touch is rubble. There must have been a rockfall since you were last here, and the opening is now blocked. You're going to have to climb down the pit.

▶ .... **GO TO** 31

107

FROM **47**

HOW TO ESCAPE?

You're a cautious person to have left those lucky charms behind. In the dim light, you cross the room, passing a casket, and reach a clay wall. It doesn't look as if there's a way out. But then you notice small holes in the wall.

Do you?

▶ Use your knife to try to cut a bigger hole in the wall .... **GO TO** 5

▶ Turn back the way you came – your knife isn't big enough to cut through all that .... **GO TO** 40

106

FROM **51**

IS THAT WHERE YOU ARE?

Studying the plan, you trace the path that you've taken. After you fell down the pit, you climbed into the storeroom, found your way through the maze, clambered from the burial chamber into the treasure room – and fell down the pit. But you see that you're only in the middle of the tomb! You're still nowhere near the entrance. Then, on the plan, you notice a cave in an annex not too far away. Maybe that's a way out!

▶ .... **GO TO** 43

Maze

Treasure Room

Burial Chamber

Pit

Cave

BIDE YOUR TIME

108

FROM 8

You wait until the tomb raiders have gone a safe distance and then climb back up the rope, out of the pit, and into the corridor. You put the rope back in your bag. Now, you use the fire drill to relight the lamp and start your journey again. The corridor narrows as you push past some large jars.

▶ GO TO 9

GATHERING EQUIPMENT

You manage to squeeze through the crack. The light is dim, but you seem to be in an old storeroom. Scattered around are dusty objects that look as if they've been there a long time. There's a rope, a knife, a chisel, a vase, a comb, a basket, a spear, a lamp, and a fire drill. These include some of the tools that tomb builders use. With a sinking feeling, you realize that you're trapped in a mummy's tomb! Some of these things could help you get out, but they won't all fit in your bag.

Which things do you put in your bag?

➤ Rope, chisel, knife, lamp .... GO TO 88

➤ Rope, knife, fire drill, lamp .... GO TO 58

➤ Rope, knife, comb, vase .... GO TO 13

TOMB BUILDERS' TOOLS

To dig tombs out of the valley rockface, builders use many tools, including chisels and ropes. To light their way through the tunnels and caverns, they need a lamp, and to light a lamp, they need a fire drill.

Rope

Oil lamp

Chisel

Fire drill

Spear

LOOK INSIDE!

110 FROM 80

With your heart beating stronger and stronger, you lean over the sarcophagus. What will you find inside? A mummy? A gruesome skeleton? Barely able to look, you keep one eye tight shut and take a quick peek inside the sarcophagus. You see …

……… GO TO 35

WHO'S THERE?

111 FROM 62

You call for help, and the voices reply that they're coming. Seconds later, three men climb through the hole you made in the wall and stumble down the piles of treasure. They don't look like a search party. They're tomb raiders. What should you do?

ASK THE EYE OF HORUS

Turn to the symbol of Uraeus.

Basket

Vase

Knife

Comb

THE DOOR OF RA

*Ra is the sun god, and very powerful. Ra rules the sky
and the Earth. Each night, Ra passes through the god
Apep's realm in the underworld before surfacing again
with the rising sun the following morning.*

THE DOOR OF APEP

*Apep is Ra's opposite and enemy. Apep is a water
serpent god who brings darkness and chaos.
Each night, Apep attempts to disrupt Ra's journey
through the underworld.*

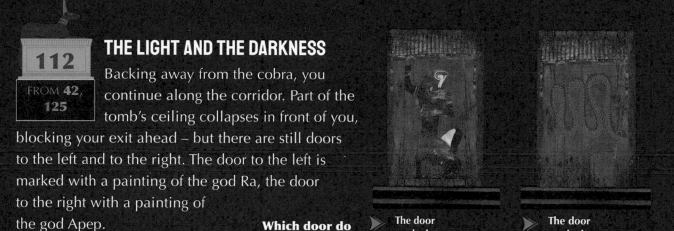

THE LIGHT AND THE DARKNESS

112

FROM **42, 125**

Backing away from the cobra, you continue along the corridor. Part of the tomb's ceiling collapses in front of you, blocking your exit ahead – but there are still doors to the left and to the right. The door to the left is marked with a painting of the god Ra, the door to the right with a painting of the god Apep.

Which door do you choose?

The door marked with Ra .... GO TO **119**

The door marked with Apep .... GO TO **67**

TERROR ALERT

113

FROM **6**

Avoiding Anubis, you climb back through the false door and are back facing the maze of corridors. But the thought of meeting rats, snakes, and that skeleton again sends a chill down your spine. You wonder, can there really be any other way out through the maze? No. You decide that you will have to face Anubis and make an offering. Taking a deep breath, you climb back through the false door and offer Anubis a honey cake from your father's lunch.

.... GO TO **116**

STUNG!

114

FROM **81**

With your bag over your shoulder, you begin to climb up the rope out of the shaft. As you climb, you feel something sting your hand.

Do you?

Shake your hand and carry on – that sting didn't hurt too much .... GO TO **27**

Climb back down the shaft and light the lamp to see what has stung you .... GO TO **46**

DEAD END

115

FROM **40**

Crawling through the low doorway, you find yourself in a small, empty room. There's no other way out and nothing here to help you. Are you going to have to crawl back out and cut through the burial chamber wall?

ASK THE EYE OF HORUS

Turn to the symbol of the Djed pillar.

THE KINGDOM OF THE DEAD

116

FROM **6,
113, 123**

You hope Anubis is satisfied with the offering you have left and step deeper into the burial chamber. Trembling a little, you look around. On the wall is a large painting of Anubis and the demon Ammit. They are working out whether the pharaoh, whose tomb you are in, led a good or a bad life. You shudder – an evil pharaoh could make this tomb a very dangerous place indeed.

WEIGHING OF THE HEART

Anubis weighs the dead pharaoh's heart. If she or he was a good person, the heart will be lighter than the feather of truth, and the pharaoh will pass freely into the afterlife. If she or he was a bad person, the heart will be weighed down with sin and eaten by the crocodile-headed monster, Ammit.

ASK THE EYE OF HORUS

Turn to the frog to discover whether this was a good or a bad pharaoh.

If you see
a feather .... GO TO 83

If you
see Ammit .... GO TO 123

FINAL ENCOUNTER

117

FROM **33**

You call out for help, hoping that this time, the tomb raiders will show mercy on you. They come charging into the hall, grab your bag, and race off into the depths of the tomb. Now, you're left in complete darkness with nothing.

▶ ····· GO TO 121

SHAKEDOWN

118

FROM **78**

Hanging from the rope in the pit, you're swinging a little. Then you feel a tugging on the rope from above. You look up – the tomb raiders have spotted you. They shake the rope violently until you fall to the bottom of the pit. Then they swing across the pit with the rope – and take it with them as they disappear from view.

▶ ·············· GO TO 73

OSIRIS

The god Osiris is known as Lord of the underworld, ruling over the realm where everyone goes when they die. If a person has been good in life, she or he is welcomed to live forever in Osiris's underworld. But if they have been bad, their heart is eaten by Ammit and their soul dies.

THE HALL OF OFFERINGS

119

FROM **71**, **112**

The door marked with Ra leads you to a small hall. On the wall is a painting of the opening of the mouth ceremony. In the middle of the hall is a stone altar where priests leave offerings. You must almost be at the tomb's entrance. You decide to make one final offering to keep the gods happy and help you escape. You open your bag on the altar.

What do you offer from your bag?

➤ Your father's lunch .... GO TO 74

➤ The fire drill .... GO TO 20

OPENING OF THE MOUTH

The opening of the mouth ceremony is the final ritual in a pharaoh's funeral. The mummy is brought to the tomb, where a priest and members of the pharaoh's family touch its mouth, ears, eyes, and nose so that it can speak and eat in the afterlife. Food is left as an offering.

RUBBLE BELOW

120

FROM **102**

You hang off the ledge from both arms and let yourself drop. Landing on the rubble now isn't too painful, but you realize you've left your lamp up on the ledge. You begin to climb across the rubble, but it very quickly gets too dark without your lamp. You are going to have to climb back up to the ledge.

➤ .... GO TO 66

OFFERINGS ON THE ALTAR
Food is left as an offering to feed the dead on their journey through the underworld.

ON ALL FOURS

121

FROM **25, 50, 117, 128**

In the darkness, you crawl across the floor, feeling your way with your hands. Something furry brushes against you, and you jump. What was that? A jackal? Or Ammit, the demon who might devour your heart?

GO TO **129**

KICKING SHINS

122

FROM **39**

You kick the tomb raider. He cries out in pain but quickly manages to tie up your feet. You clench your fists before he binds your hands together.

GO TO **29**

BAD PHARAOH

123

FROM **116**

You're in the tomb of a bad pharaoh and in huge danger. Or are you?

GO BACK TO **116**

DESPERATE EFFORTS

124

FROM **73**

You try again to build a ramp out of the pit, but again, it slips away from under you and you fall back to the bottom. This is hopeless. You're going to have to try to climb up the walls.

GO TO **26**

A PRAYER

125

FROM **42**

You read out the prayer, but the snake keeps slithering toward you.

Do you?

Carefully back away from the cobra ⋯⋯⋯ GO TO **112**

Consider yourself protected by the spell and jump past the cobra ⋯⋯ GO TO **37**

LIGHTING THE LAMP

126

FROM **16, 45, 58, 79, 94**

You've watched your mother light a fire drill many times before – now you need to remember how to do it.

With the lamp lit, you make your way back across the room and head toward an opening in the opposite wall.

▶ .... **GO TO** **85**

Bow

HOW TO USE A FIRE DRILL

1. Make sure the drill is set up correctly.
2. Push and pull the bow back and forth to make the drill turn.
3. Tear off a small piece of fabric from your tunic. Then, when a burning spot appears in the notch at the base of the drill, hold the fabric to it.
4. Light the fabric from the burning spot and then use the fabric to light the lamp oil. Success!

Drill   *Notch*

THE TWO GODDESSES

127

FROM **24**

The Eye of Horus leads you into the corridor of the flood season. The corridor soon reaches a fork. One is marked by a picture of a vulture and the other by a picture of a cobra. You know that these represent the goddesses Nekhbet and Wadjet.

Which corridor do you choose?

➤ Nekhbet the vulture .... **GO TO** 100

➤ Wadjet the cobra .... **GO TO** 2

NOTHING LEFT

128

FROM **74**

You blow the lamp out and hide behind the altar. From there, you can just see the tomb raiders approach. Spotting the lamp and your bag, they take both and race off, arguing about where next to look for treasure. You're left in complete darkness.

➤ .... **GO TO** 121

WADJET
The goddess Wadjet is often shown as a cobra. She protects Lower Egypt.

NEKHBET
The goddess Nekhbet is shown as a vulture. She protects Upper Egypt, where you live.

129

A CHINK OF LIGHT

Crawling in the darkness, you're scared the animal that brushed against you might bite. You feel the corners of a doorway and reach another room. There's a chink of light at the other end of it. Could this be the entrance hall to the tomb? Are you almost free? You can just see the pointed ears of what you think brushed against you – it's a cat, only a cat.

The cat jumps across boulders up toward the light and disappears through it. You follow, but the hole is much too small for you to climb through. But through it, you can see the valley outside. You're almost free!

Do you?

➤ Try to dig your way out
with your bare hands .... **GO TO** 53

➤ Cry for help
through the hole .... **GO TO** 64

130

FROM 93

HELP!

You shout out for help, but no one answers and no one comes.

Do you?

➤ Try to climb back
up the shaft .... **GO TO** 98

➤ Attempt to climb
through the crack .... **GO TO** 109

THE TRUE PATH THROUGH THE TOMB!

To get out of the tomb safely and in the shortest number of steps, you need to take the true path. To do that, judge each option carefully and use the clues in the pictures and captions to help you. If you get stuck, see the answers below.

(1) Rockfall! Go to 93

(2) Where Are You?
Try to climb through the crack in the wall. No one can hear you shout and the shaft is blocked, so there's no point in climbing back up. Go to 109

(3) Gathering Equipment
Take the rope, knife, lamp, and fire drill. You need the fire drill to light the lamp. Without the lamp, you can't see your way through the dark tomb.
Go to 58

(4) Into the Darkness Go to 126

(5) Lighting the Lamp
Go to 85

(6) The Maze
You should risk jumping over the rats. They may bite, but the bite won't kill you. You may die on the other paths through the maze. Go to 28

(7) A False Door
You have to pull yourself up and crawl through the hole in the door. You won't be able to smash a hole in the base of it. Go to 6

(8) The Guard Dog
You should step past Anubis, but only after making an offering of food. Anubis is a hugely powerful god, and people show their respect to Anubis by leaving offerings of food in tombs. Go to 116

(9) The Kingdom of the Dead Go to 83

(10) Look Up! Go to 4

(11) Goddess of the Sky
The star pattern with an even number of stars includes the brightest star Sopdet. Go to 80

(12) A Broken Sarcophagus
Yes, dare to look inside the sarcophagus. It might be scary, but it's not disrespectful.
Go to 110

(13) Look Inside! Go to 35

(14) A Face in the Dark
Take a closer look at the face in the dark. It won't hurt you. Go to 92

15 Mystery of the Coffins Go to 47

16 Lucky Charms
Leave the amulets. They won't bring you any luck. Go to 107

17 How to Escape
Use your knife to try to cut a hole in the wall. It's the only way you can move forward in the tomb. Go to 5

18 A Bright Light Go to 75

19 A Glint of Gold Go to 52

20 Finders, Keepers
Leave the treasures where they are. Priests put curses on people who steal from tombs, and if the thieves are caught, they are executed. Go to 59

21 Pharaoh for a Day
The white crown is the crown of Upper Egypt, where you live. Go to 22

22 The Royal Bed Go to 62

23 Woken from a Dream Keep quiet and listen, because you don't want the tomb raiders to find you. They're violent and won't help you. Go to 72

24 Strange Voices
Hide behind the bed. It's best that the tomb raiders never see you. Go to 95

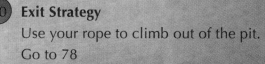

25 A Hidden Opening Go to 63

26 A Hanging Rock Go to 97

27 Down the Pit Go to 51

28 A Gift from the Dead Go to 106

29 Is That Where You Are? Go to 43

30 Exit Strategy
Use your rope to climb out of the pit. Go to 78

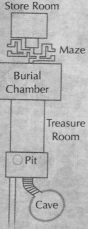

31 Rope Tricks
Slip down to the bottom of the rope so the tomb raiders don't see you. Go To 8

32 Raiders Again Go To 108

33 Bide Your Time Go To 9

34 Fire! Fire! Go To 18

Store Room

Maze

Burial Chamber

Treasure Room

Pit

Cave

35 A Choice of Direction
Turn left to find the cave in the annex. When you looked at the plan, you thought there might be a shortcut out that way. Go To 91

36 Enter the Annex
The rubble is too difficult to clamber across, so climb up onto the ledge to cross the cave. Go To 54

37 Along the Ledge Go To 102

38 Meet the Dead
Push past the mummies. They may look horrible, but they're harmless. Go to 86

39 Hanging On
Try to pull yourself back up onto the ledge. It's difficult, but it's better than falling down onto the rubble. Go to 66

40 End of the Cave Go to 101

41 Out of Fuel
Go back to the corridor to look for oil in the jars. You seem to remember seeing some there. Go to 44

42 Going Back
You've heard a snake hiss and there might be one in the jars. A snake bite could be deadly, but it's worth the risk, and you decide to put your hand inside the jar. Go to 49

43 Reaching In
Climb down to the pit to check the jars there for lamp oil. Go to 31

THE EYE OF HORUS

The Eye of Horus wheel on the front cover is the keeper of symbols. It will help you to find out where to go next on your journey through the tomb. Discover what the symbols mean below.

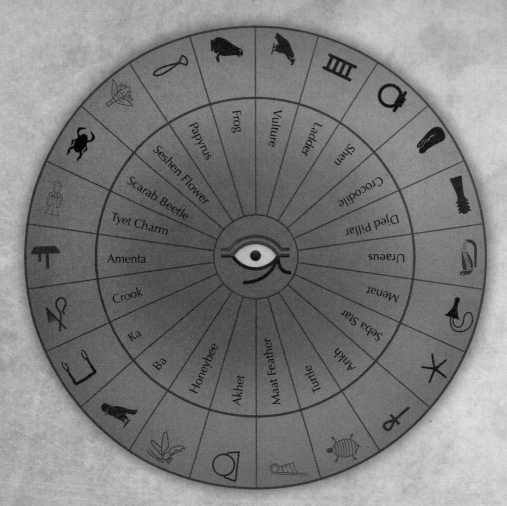

The scarab beetle is a lucky charm.

A Tyet charm protects the wearer from evil.

The Amenta means land of the dead.

The Ka is the symbol for life force.

The Ba represents the spirit of a person who flies to the next world.

The flower of the Seshen is a symbol of rebirth.

Honeybees are symbols of royalty.

The ladder allows the god Osiris to reach the starry sky.

The Ankh is a good luck charm.

The Maat feather represents truth.

The Seba star represents the souls of the dead.

The Shen is a loop of rope, a symbol everlasting life.

The Akhet is a good luck charm.

The papyrus stem represents youth and strength.

The Menat is a symbol of life and joy.

The Uraeus cobra is a symbol of royal power.

The Djed pillar is a symbol of stability.

The shepherd's crook represents kingship.

The frog is a symbol of birth.

The vulture is protector of the Egyptian pharaohs.

The turtle brings bad luck.